Mercy

Mercy

Dvorah Simon

Hanford Mead Publishers, Inc.
Santa Cruz, California

FIRST EDITION

ISBN 13: 978-1-59275-011-5 (alk. paper)

ISBN 10: 1-59275-011-7 (alk. paper)

Manufactured in the United States of America

This edition is printed on Ph neutral paper that meets the American National Standards Institute Z39.48 Standard.

10 9 8 7 6 5 4 3 2 1

Cover credit: "The Victory of Mercy" (Evelyn Beatrice Longman), photo by Lee Sandstead. www.sandstead.com

CONTENTS

Foreword

There is a mountain in Tibet, high in the Himalayan mountains, that is used for an intensive ritual in the Tibetan tradition. A pilgrim on a spiritual journey walks the circumference of the mountain—one path takes about four days, the other about three times that long. The solitary trek climbs through fairly high elevations, beset frequently with inclement weather and other challenging conditions. But the completion of the journey is said to transform one's consciousness in deep ways. As the ritual circle is completed, an awareness arises that the mountain is within you, that fields of consciousness are all around you. This knowledge is indeed wondrous and healing.

In this stunning book of poems that you hold in your hands, Dvorah Simon will take you through a similar trek of transformation. To open to the human dimension is to open to many different experiences: the ache of longing, the desire for surrender, the awe of transcendence, the call for healing, and the enchantment of creative imagination, to name but a few. All of these threads whisper their incantations in the weave of Dvorah's poems. She shows a startling capacity and willingness to sink to the depths of darkness, open her heart to absorb some alchemical lead of the human psyche, and then give birth to a poem that transmutes it into the gold of fully human consciousness. For this we can all be grateful and encouraged.

Stephen Gilligan, Ph.D.

Preface

Once upon a time, there was a little girl who wrote a poem about the moon. Over the years, there were more poems – some about the moon, and some about other things.

Writing poetry is an act of inquiry, as well as an act of love. One enters the poem with no compass, no map at all, hoping and waiting for surprise and revelation. Inquiry requires the sensed presence of another, whether that other is a voice from within, an intuition of mystery, or a specific embodied form. The process of inquiry requires both tenderness and discipline; tenderness for the murmur that arises from consciousness—attended to and cherished, and discipline to shape that murmur into words. Such shaping has great power, for once named, a thing is forever transformed, whether it is brought further into consensual reality by that naming, or released from an ancient and unyielding form, free to dissipate and evolve. Words rise up from silence, from chaos, from dream – from bone and earth, stone and rain, from the half-heard word in another room, from the dream you wake with the feeling of but can't quite recall. To hold these things in the hands of your imagination, at once expecting nothing and waiting for them to reveal themselves to you, is an act of faith – the faith that the inquiry will yield something, even though that thing may not have existed prior to the moment in which it was called, by your question, into being.

Most of the poems in this book were written in the last dozen or so years, and are a meditation on mercy; mercy to others, mercy to self, mercy to the voices within that rumble and roar, are ugly or beautiful, are harsh or kind. Each section of the book attends to a different energy within that meditation – the energies of passion and faith, death and transcendence, creativity, the cycles of nature and time, and finally, mercy.

Many people have nurtured this project, calling it into being with affection and faith; most especially, Ruth Crickard, Barb Geiger, and Stephen Gilligan. They have my deepest thanks. Thanks also to my mother, Magda Simon, for reading me Milne and writing down that poem about the moon (I was not yet lettered), and to my sister, Julie Simon, for the music she brought and still brings to my life. I would also like to thank the following people for their encouragement and support over the course of many years: Louisa Yap, Lisa Croner, Larry Goldstein, Patricia Casamo, Susan Egelko, David Gaines, Rose Lynn Sherr, Donna Langenbahn, Sandra Koppit Cohen, Lee Orlando, Pattie Sisson, Valerie Watts, Patricia Houser, Rhiannon Shaw, Clif Bullard, Ann Blessing, Janice Pessar, Leonie Nowitz, Yvonne Dolan, Loraine Masterton, Selene Vega, Irene Cornish, Cindy Lamprecht, Brian McKay, Richard Clark, and Janis Knight. Thanks especially to Barb Geiger and Janis Knight again, along with Roberto Weisz and Jenny McKnight, for their invaluable feedback on the manuscript. A warm thank you to Kylea Taylor, for her faith in this project. Finally, this book is dedicated to the memory of two Williams: William Arsenault, who taught me that "artists are the healers of society" and who made me promise I'd publish someday, and J. William Whedbee, whose love for the Song of Songs was lived in his unstinting espousal of a life that was at once spiritual and passionate.

1

The Passion Road

~ *To travel it, prepare to throw good sense away*

Unspeak Me

Unspeak me,
if that's what it takes
to mold me to Your Name

Sinew by sinew,
unmake me;
taking me apart,
make me Yours

Unmask me,
all the shadow selves,
that, hissing and growling,
keep me
from Your side

Unname me, down to
nothing, no-one,
neverwas.
until there is only,
ever,
Your breath

Only undone,
in this density of
being,
can I hope to learn
no beginning
and no end

And only unspoken
can I stand,

upon my blood and bone,
this life—
unspeakably apart
from You

PSALM

No future.
The past is a story or a dream.
An excuse. A confession.

How shall I praise You?
With what liturgy?

My body strains to call Your name,
in its alphabet of breathing,
its alphabet of blood.

You are elusive.
When you kiss me,
I struggle awake,
only to find
a whisper of your shadow.

You are
a forgotten tenderness
I would sacrifice all hope
to remember.

THE AGE OF SUSTAINED CONTRADICTIONS

This is the age of sustained contradictions.

The year I stopped talking to God.
The year I felt his breath on my neck.
The year I felt her in my most uncomfortable parts.
Everything can and will be taken from you,
everything you think you are.
Everything can and will be given to you,
everything else.

Equanimity struggles with desire, and smiles,
the princess on the windowsill.
Windows call louder, "Fly! Fly!"

The soul You gave me: untouchable, whole.
The soul I carry, torn.

With which soul's wings
will I fly?

THE PASSION ROAD

The passion road:
to travel it,
prepare to fling
good sense away,
but do not fling it away.
Prepare to bleed,
but carry closely,
along with your thorns,
the child of your desire.

Tears? Yes.
Joy and sadness and
suffering suffused.
Always reaching,
always out of reach.

For that moment of fire,
this pain,
gladly.

INANNA

Softly
a secret treasure
rises in my blood, singing

until my ears are buzzing
and sun pours through
my weakened limbs

How can I know this as myself?
Thunderous shadows,
shattering dreams,

the mad descant of ancient grief,
released, and the sundering relief
of the broken thing

Here, in as many nows as hearing names,
as sight can parse,
only my breath whispers around me,
ungoverned, unforgiven, whole

Vision dark and true, I rise,
rapt in my own
descent

BLOSSOMING

There is a dark
blossoming: pain and
fear arise and

throw me off my game.
Are you messengers?
Warnings?

Whispering, they beckon:
no translation but into
light. Without rhythm, without

remorse, I pose my final question,
awkwardly: will you....?
The whispering subsides

and all I can do is wait.
Nothing left. I choose.
Surrendering, I am born again

to darkness, and received.
I close my eyes:
safely bundled, safely wrapped.

Here in this dark,
the whispers begin again.

Only now,
they are saying:
Welcome.

The Sleeping Angel

Delicately you rewrite
the stories that bind me
to darkness and pain.

You do not wipe the slate,
but rather, cherish.

The broken thing awakes;
The sleeping angel
rises into light.

               ∼ *for J.C.B.*

TAKEN

This time she is unprepared.
The heat rides her,
uncoiling like a wind, an intelligent wind
blasting her from her heart, her groin —

She watches, from very far away
as she is taken.

After, she will kneel and kiss
the fragrant earth,
fingers passing love back
into the ground.

SONG OF A SHY LOVER

Will you kiss me?
Why?

Will you drink me? My essence
in small droplets on your lips?
Will you taste me?

Will you bite me? Touch me? Tease me?

Will you kiss me to ignite me
with your fire?
Will you call my fire out?

And if I kiss you back,
inflamed and hungry like a child,
will you receive me?

Will you sooth me?
Or send me deeper,
inescapably, irretrievably
into fire?

ANNUNCIATION

All the ice in the world
won't cool me down
when you come to me
with that fire in your eyes.

Am I the burning bush?
All my life
I've offered myself
as tinder for another's flame.

When the fire burned down,
what remained?

You, sweet you,
you lick at me,
sparks flare,
and the heat rises, igniting,
but I am not consumed.

Be careful where we walk,
Beloved.
It is holy ground.

STRONG AS BONE

The way the hair pin tangles
in her hair, and she has to stop
and carefully pull it out.

Her lower lip purses, and her eyes go
so she cannot see you.
Such a small thing,
such a small, small thing
this is, and yet it opens in you
such a small place, a gap,
a catch, breathing.

Without looking as if you are anything
but casual, you watch,
waiting for her
return.

Resonant/Naming

Is it only out loud
That a thing is truly said?
What of the whisper,
time-trapped, of a thing
spoken once, and then remembered?

What of the room inside the words
inside a poem?

Like the hollow of a woman's throat,
when you run your finger down it.

The way she swallows, and breathes, slowly,
through your touch,
and turns her eyes to you.

Caught in her gaze you realize
it is you who resonates with the passion
she has borne,
and she who by her body names
your wakening desire.

PULSE

The rhythm is true, like
breathing, like waves. Listen with your bones,
let your gut respond, clenching, and in pain;
drenched in bliss.

Drumming is the Root.
Poetry, ecstasy, sex, it all derives
from the silky fluency of your skin,
the metered perfection of your brow,
the riddled canticle of your pulse.

Enter me, sublime,
as words enter time,
as poetry, the mind.
Break against me like a sea,
'till there is nothing left
of me.

THERE IS A KIND OF WORD

There is a kind of word
that rides within,
that hisses on my breath,
sparks midnight error in my brain,
thumps against my heart
drips teasingly down my leg —
tears of pleasure...

There is a kind of pausing,
listening as a sensory load,
listening for that word,
that speaks tellingly of grace,
and spirits laughing
behind the masks our bodies dream.

I would speak that word to you,
if only I could hear its potent
whisper, its steadfast pulse.
Stretching, I reach inside
until the dark consumes me,
until the light is born and spoken
in a word:

The word is always, only:
Love.

Receiving the Sabbath

Music plays me,
as if my body were the reed
the Player blows.

The sound, sweet and high,
pierces me to the core,
and I am undone.

I hold myself, uncertain of the propriety
of my response.
All around me people smile
and sway and sing in harmonies.

Blessedly, relief comes
in the form of a minor key.
No more of that nostalgia,
the cruelty of happiness, that
almost-memory of God.

Something unwinds inside,
the knot unfolds.
My breath goes further
inside my body. Ancient, ancient,
I can hear this, the sound of prophecy,
the shouting of angels, undone, so undone,
I can almost remember.

In the sound of mourning, comfort.
In the melodies of grief,
a riven peace.

Sometimes,
the hardest thing to bear
is love.

How to Pray

A woman's power: hard or soft?
Power and authority are not the same:
authority is power that is recognized,
that can be pointed to and named.

Never let it be said
that women have no power.
What man can resist
the lure of infinite softness?

Nevertheless I find myself both yang and yin,
mistress of both mercy and of sin.
Sink deep, let me sink deep or, you,
sink deep in me. Who controls?

Can we put enough bounds on what we do that
animals and otherness, dark things and wind
    and rain and song
will be content to arrive through us
and meet each other through each other's eyes?

You must pledge this guardianship with me or I will
    not engage.
I am interested neither in some bland, safe, and
    surface enactment
of man and woman joined nor in an unbounded,
    unnamed,
and unclaimed release; rather,

I do pledge, with you, a co-equal trust in madness;
    in water, fire and grief.
Let us guard each other and ourselves;

let us call each other by our truer names: Goddess,
    God, or slave,
father, mother, child, furred thing, beast:

Lover. Divinely joyous, madly and animally true.
Shyly, I reveal to you my shyest smile.
In the drumbeat of my blood,
trembling and alive, I reach for you...

In the darkness you unlock the deepest music that
    my body makes;
an ocean of ageless suffering finds release
and we, with tenderness amidst the pain
whisper prayers into each other's mouths.

TEA

First a green leaf, waves
in a sun of shadows. We
scald it: feel its bloom.

So, you came to me
as one young in leaf. Still, etched
upon your spirit,

Aroma of the
burning. Wisdom, I wanted.
There was more, you said.

Ordinary man.
No, never that. And when the
fire came between, I

cried in rage against
your lies. Still. Here I am now,
torn, awake, in wait,

wishing we were free
of tales that trap our souls. I
want you in my arms.

Teeth upon your flesh.
With mercy or with none, I'll
suck you scent and leaf.

THE AGE OF PERFECTION

This is the age of perfection:
heartache, sagging skin,
a less redoubtable cleverness,
bones in ardent protest
of morning's tender cruelty,
and all the long regret
of passion leashed,
and all the times I did
the sensible thing.

What grace could rival this?
To know these scars
mark one who has survived,
and name, with wary harumph
the queen of pain.

Come, subjects, and
make obeisance.
I will tutor you all
in wisdom and disdain.

Did you treasure your desire,
or failing that, choose peace?
Taste it: it is your fruit.
What part of yourself did you kill
to stay alive?

WHEN YOU TOLD ME

When you told me you felt
a sterility in your life,
I wanted to take you
and smear pomegranates across your lips.

Swollen and red, your mouth would be ripe
for kisses.
I can see you, a little alarmed,
your hand cupping the rounded curves
of your mound.

Don't take yes for an answer, my dear.
No, not the yeses of modern life
in its inexcusable ennui.

It's easy to see that "no" is not right.
It's the yeses you have to watch out for,
the yeses that lull you, that creep into your sleep,
that say, yes, it's all right, your shallow breathing,
your quiet intolerable desiccation,
nothing more to see here, just sink into it,
no one will notice, not even you.

Can you taste what I am telling you?
Are your fingers crushing, even now,
those red, red seeds?

It will stain, you know.

LIKING THE DEVIL

And it's the longing itself, she said –

tendrils of, and shivers, and the mid-day
spill of luscious, mmmm,
reach for... squirm just that
centimeter off-key and it
cascades to shoulders, to neck,
shooting straight up, oh glory, oh shit –

the longing itself that chimes me on.

And he was there, smiling, catching it all,
letting it rumble through him in a laugh,
shaping sound into a tool of becoming,
making it all mean something.
Calling the chaos, giving it form.
An electric dance of wind and pain,
frustration and desire.

It's the longing I love,
she said,

as the storm,
without his word to bind it,
grew frittery and close.

CIPHER

There was a time
I was encrypted in your smile
and every resonance of you
bespoke me.

Then living
broke the code.
The harmony dispersed,
and I was left wondering
how I ever sang that song.

I have a song to sing, now,
a song for you. But it's one
you'll never hear. Too strange,
and I never knew, how dissonant
the cipher of your pain.

MEN LIE

Men lie.
They are incapable
of doing otherwise.

The harder they try
to tell the truth,
the more sweat
pops out of their heads,
their hearts start to flutter
and fear raises its claws,
sinking into them.

Then, then, they are at
their most dangerous.
In rage at their own terror
they will lash out.

Step back
and let the maelstrom pass.
Their glazed eyes will see
only threat, and not you.
Step back,
and let the maelstrom pass.

Nor hope, ever, for the truth.
The truth, don't you know,
is very dangerous.

Sing, then,
a lullaby, a charm.

Be feminine, be yielding.
Let the lie rise between you,
once again.
Hold him, rocked asleep,
against your bosom, while you
sing the praises
of his fearlessness, his power,
and his strength.

In the Hollow

You came to me in the hollow
of the thing that had to leave

than despair, the hollow made
by the things that leave —
whispers, crusts, and dreams.

I cried when they left
but it had to be.
I had to be emptied out
before I'd let you in.

As if the wind itself
had a name in the emptied house,
and quieter than shock,
you were there,
a small hum of vibration
casually leaking through.

You came to me in the hollow
of the things that had to leave.
The maybes, the almosts, the neverweres,
the charms of a reasonable life, released,
releasing me so I could find, jagged and raw as n
unhealed bone,
the ache I have for You.

What About Them?

Noticing an audience
I turn to Him.

"What about them?" I ask, gesturing.
"They seem... eager, or something."

I am not sure what I am supposed to do.
These whispers and rants

were the very definition of private,
my insidest insides.

He roars and I step back, unthinking,
as if there is a "forward" or a "back", here.

He's almost choking, like a hacking cough.
Dawningly, I realize it's laughter.

This goes on for a while, long enough
for my own breathing to settle down.

Finally he finishes in a little happy wheeze.

"Did you think you could speak my Name,"
he says, "and no one would hear?"

Be Careful

I once saw a movie, a French movie
in which a young girl finds a man.
He's a kind, interesting man, a boy, really,
who pledges his love for her.
He's a little mad, but in a romantic,
French movie way:
He tapes the sound of her name,
and plays it to himself as he walks around,
as he rides a bus, as he goes about his way,
the tape player hidden in his coat,
and coming out from it, over and over,
like a litany, her name.

Having nothing to *his* name,
he goes away for a year, to make his fortune,
so he can return, and be worthy of her love.

In the meantime another man finds her,
a deep and cruel man.
A man who rips the clothes from her back
and the dignity from her soul,
who stirs the beast inside,
who sucks and kicks and growls,
and brings her to do the same.
A violent man. She never knows
which way his hand will fall.

She hates this man. But it's too late.
He's taken the thing she had to give,
her passion, and her dreams.

When the young man, the kind young man returns,
she sadly greets him with a smile.
Somewhere in her heart is a place where he belongs,
but she can't go back;
She is unable to leave the one who bonded her
to his flesh.
Be careful who you love.

THE END OF POETRY

Your breath is the end of poetry.
There were days on end.
There was the length of you,
warm at my back.

I drank you like a potion.
Kisses were words you spoke to my skin,
an incantation of mercy.

Caged in a binding of your desire,
I unfolded into you.
Flowing, demanding,
your touch, your breath.

And within me,
fire and torment and peace.

Now
you are gone.
Time again
for words.

In Praise of the Bitter Seed

There is a time for laughing. Falling down,
head back, your middle unprotected.
"No, stop," you cry,
but you go deeper into your drowning,
sliding backward, gliding further
into it.

Release.

There is a time for pain. Slow implosion,
a hardening.
Throat clenched, whiplashed breath.
Choking on it, afraid to fall.
"No, stop," you cry,
but you go deeper, as if bound,
once the thing, the thing that gives you pain
is known.

Witness.

And here we are,
betwixt.
Last week you woke me
with kisses.
This week I strain to hear you.
Tell me again
how you miss
the way I tasted on your tongue?

Memory betrays us. Teases us with guesses.
An impudent feather, tickling
hunger, joy, and grief.

We'll live like this, awhile,
you in your place, I in mine.

You tend to your house and write your notes.
I comb my hair and sing
songs in praise of the bitter seed.

CHAIN LETTER

You bind me
as a sign upon your heart;
a secret scroll
foretells our end:

Love, unbound,
comes upon us,
undoes the mystery
of our joining,
releases us to choose,
freely, for the first time.

Can we stand the light, real light
in each other's eyes?
Or are we ruined
without our chains?

KISSING THE CHAINS

clear blue window in a
castle wall

the way out is clear,
but not the way on

caught between my freedom,
and kissing the chains

I stand, gaping,
at the summer sky

PRIORITIES

What is this wounding I daily invite,
daily taste deeply on my tongue like
clandestine wine, stolen, and so,
drunk jealously, and in haste?
Here, in my breast, see it:
my beating heart. How you tutored it
to skip for you.
I play you its syncope,
though you have long since
stopped your ears
with the daily tutelage
of prior devotions.
Still, you smile at me.
You even extend a hand,
and, fool that I am,
smiling sweetly, I take it.

FORBIDDEN FIRE

You're the forbidden fire in my life.
Should I walk away,
or stay here, risking burning?

Cold, cold, cold,
without you.
Even if there's nothing but ash,
if I stay.

HITLER FUCKED THE EARTH

Hitler fucked the earth
and my body was born.
Dancing deep in each cell
the dirt of his vile shadow
and perverse revelation.

Hitler fucked the earth
And deep gashes bled,
a rainbow of seeds
sprouting in the grooves,
the furrows dark with blood and filth,

and my body my body my body
was born.

Touch it, and I scream.
So sexual, so charged.
The kundalini snake has no kindnesses for me,
it takes me harshly, choking me by the neck,
down to the ground.
I am coughing in the filth of it,
breathing in his seed,
inhaling and hacking up my blood
to further soak this holy ground.

Long ago someone chose.
Chose me as an offering and
the earth received me
and I agreed
and now, only now

do I see the choice I made.
Dark gift that merited nothing,
that cherished nothing, only to be reviled
and yet,
holy nonetheless.
For is my allegiance, then,
worth nothing?

Would that this god would die,
and another take me.
I am very well trained
to the yoke.

ALL FALL DOWN

been there, felt that
put the ashes in a hat
want to die but that's okay
have to live another day

been that, felt there,
washed the ashes from my hair,
want to sing but got it stuck
trying so hard to give a fuck

been felt, that there
is the thing that isn't fair
breathing hard but that's okay
going to scream another day

WHERE THEY LIVE

I'd like to write some pretty poems
but a nightmare is writhing in my gut.

I'm suspicious of anger, yet here I am,
seething.

How to drop into an honesty of feeling
without losing my hold on a higher commitment to
Love?

Down. Silly child. Settle down.
Only I am afraid of falling.

I'll curl up, here, around this hurt.
I'll nurse this barb of fury, and keep the sensitive
places

well guarded,
well away.

Be careful not to look me in the eye too closely,
dear.

I'm not at all safe to be around. Not unless
you don't mind a bruise or two.

Bang it up, bang it up on
holy ground.

Not unless, my friend,
you have monsters in your belly too.

Fingering the Curse

Flayed, he stands, not without some pride:
to survive is prize enough.
He stares at his hands, grimy with dark residue.
They will never be clean. The curse is real.
Nevertheless, he feels the power
his surrender grants him.
Even in their contempt,
he sees the fear in their eyes,
the narrowing as they look, and back away.

They know they could never live this pain.
It isn't much, but it's his, this victory.
Claiming it, he laughs. His head thrown back
against the bellowing wind, he laughs until his face
is stained with tears against the grime.
So painted, he readies himself for the next
arriving blows.

ALPHABEATEN

Abattoirs,
Blood,
Carnage,
Doom,
Escape
Forbidden,
Gone to
Hell,
Immolated,
Jaundiced,
Kerosene-
Laden,
Mangled,
Noosed,
Oppressed, and
Parboiled.
Quests repealed.
Rancid,
Shitted on,
Tortured,
Unfulfilled,
Vented,
Wasted,
eXsanguinated,
Yellow-bellied
Zombied, zeroized zit.

KNIFE

Your desire for me
is a knife in my belly.
I watch in slow motion
as the slice is made.
Blood wells; it answers
your demand.
You step close,
and bring the taste
of my passion
to your lips.

Beaten Track

FBI agent music, killer music,
lost children songs,
all of it.

Throw it at me. Let it flare
within and marry through the
song inside to darkness.

I will spell it, then.
Spell you, and won't you be wishing,
then, you'd listened
to the warning label.

~for Rhi

An Entirely Different Angel

Sometimes we seek
a bad thing.

And sometimes, it is like an addiction.
An almost satisfaction.
Redemption without consciousness,
circling over and over,
with marginal variations —
just enough to keep you hooked.

And there is a lot of investment,
and drama, and pride, and each take
is more convincing than the last:
only a little farther, this time,
and the wound will be healed.

But the wound is not healed.

But sometimes, another thing occurs,
a true thing; Maya's treasure.
Willing chains that are a womb of awakening.

The way Israel had to go down to slavery,
to Egypt, to be born, out of the narrow places,
out of the waters of the sea.

Sometimes,
we choose a bad thing,
a time of lying in the earth. Of blindness,
of subjugation. Obeisance to a dark lord,
or to darker imaginings.

Sometimes, there is sacrifice, and pain,
and glory in it, and shame,
and a terrible release, and the sudden, searing fire
of awareness, in which the old nightmare
is finally named, and brought forth, and claimed,
almost as a lost child, given up so long before,
we've forgotten the light of its birth,
but only kept the pain.
And in this confluence, finally,
of self and self,
your voice is heard.
You come into your desire, and name it "good."
The hidden spark is released from the prison
in which, hidden,
it could only be seen as monstrous.
Free, it floats, lightly, an entirely different angel,
and you are touched, with blessing,
with an almost unbearable regard,
and there is something musical, but it is not music.
And something inside, something in you,
that has not smiled for a very long time,
smiles.

But all this, of course, is lies.

The truth is a thousand times more delicate,
more joyous, and more grave.

2

Words Rise Up from Silence

~ *Some days, going up in smoke is the only way to rise*

AKEDA FROM THE OTHER SIDE*

Binding himself, he lays his body down
against the stone, the sun's slanting rays
pinning his eyelids nearly shut.

His head back, he relaxes,
and waits.

The stone is cold,
a deep cold from the night
and it seeps into his bones.

Pale gold is the morning light,
sharp but not enough to warm.
Nevertheless he knows
the fire that is to come.

Readying himself,
he surrenders deeper into the harsh light,
the cold stone, finding his way,
finding his peace —

to find it sundered
by such clownish theatre
as only God and his father can devise:

Loudly, a ram bleats in the bushes
a terrible release.

** Akeda is the Hebrew term for what is usually translated as the
"binding" of Isaac in preparation for his sacrifice by his father
at the behest of God. The meaning of the Hebrew word is in fact
closer to something like a trussing or a hog-tie.*

Isaac:
Words Rise Up From Silence

How can I admit I enjoyed the feel
of my father's blade against my neck?

I was ready.
I had a heart of love.

And now, here I am,
in a sacrificed world,

walking with the measured steps
of post-angelic destiny.

I didn't ask for this freedom,
but here it is, beneath the shattered stones
I'm standing on.

In the thicket,
that damnable ram.

GOING UP IN SMOKE

Some days, going up in smoke
is the only way to
rise.

(Above your circumstance? Above the pain?)

Stand, feet planted in the fire.
There's much to lose but
Everything to gain.

protected in Eternal flame

AKEDA, ANNOTATED

After an untold number of years
he finds God in the most unexpected place.

Perhaps it's a social security office,
and God is a clerk.
Or the Korean woman giving you a pedicure.

"I have," God says, "many names."

With the mystery of hidden angels
flickering blindly into his eyes,
he reminds himself, belatedly,
to breathe.

Once rhythm is regained
he remembers anger, too.

It takes a few tries but he musters
everything he ever had to ask his question.

"What" he says,
his voice barely human above
the rage, "was that about?"

God sighs, not without
compassion in His eyes.
The love is so fierce
the man cowers as if he's been struck.
Another sigh, and this, too, is gentled.

"I know you suffered."

A pause. "Is that the best you can do?"

"I suppose it's fair to want more..."

The man, surprised, squints into the light.

"It was," God says,
"a qualified failure. I wanted, you see,
for them to understand –
it's not sacrifice I desire, but life.

"For you to live your lives, all of you,
in joy and love.
Why else did I make you? Why else did I make you
as you are? With all your precious ordinary needs.

"I didn't know how else to let them know.
Except to take them, take him, your father,
to the very brink of all I wanted him to deny."

The man listens quietly, anger dulled
in a daze of disbelief.
After all this time.

Shadows fly across the sun and clear.
Rain washes air and earth. Wind abates
and rises yet again.

The man realizes he is hungry, and has to pee.
Getting up, he slowly makes his way
out of the office, down to the street.

Vaguely realizing that someone is following
he turns back and slowly makes out his quiet
companion.

"How long have you been with me?"

God smiles. "All the time."

"A kind of psychodrama. That's what it was?"

God nods. "A qualified failure," he repeats.
"They didn't exactly get the clue. All this
needless..."

God sweeps his hand.

"....suffering."

"What about my blessing?" Isaac says.
"You blessed my father but the angel,"
and here he indulges in a maudlin sniff,
"had no word for me."

God pulls him to Himself.
"What greater love," He whispers to his soul,
"than to release you to your life?
Let life define your life,
not the tyranny of stones.
Let that mountain be the last altar
you'll lay yourself upon.
Breathe freedom. Be an ordinary man.

And smile your gladness now and then.
It's prayer enough, and all I need."

The man awakes.
There's quiet where he's dwelled in pain
so long he'll need a lexicon of joy
to school him to his reborn ways.

We leave him now, and wave.
And smile our gladness now and then.
It's prayer enough, and all we need.

THE RIVER

My father is dreaming of a river.
"I was sleeping," he says. "And I felt that if I woke,
I'd be in the house in Delaware where we lived,
and all I had to do
was look out the window,
and see the river."

I knew you couldn't see the river
from that house.
I said, "you are going through your life."
He said, "I am moving around in time."

He's sleeping a lot.
He's almost awake.
We used to go down to the river
in old New Castle, where William Penn landed,
and small, neat Dutch houses stand.

I rode my bike to the river with Louisa.
We had to pass the railroad tracks
and the War Memorial.
We passed our fort in the woods, and
Dead Man's Tree.

But my father's river
is not beyond the tracks, or the War,
or the Tree.

Those things
are behind him now.
And the River
is calling him home.

WHITE CROW

That night,
his relatives come to me in a dream,
one female, one male.
We are in a diner, in a booth.
We are all very relaxed.

"It's okay," they say.
"Everything is all right. He's
with us now."

I wake up comforted. It lingers
for days.

After the funeral,
there is a white crow.
In the dream, I ask,
"What the hell does a white crow mean?"
Even so, I know it is from, or about, my Dad.

A woman steps up to a microphone.
"In dreams," she intones,
"a white crow signifies faith."

Well, duh.

A week passes, more.
I come home early from work,
still jet-lagged.
Falling asleep with my clothes on I dream
he's not dead after all, but somehow alive again.
But still sick, still lingering.

Disappointed, complaining.
There is no escape.

And again, a place where someone is giving me
small items, ancient but tiny books and scrolls.
I am not sure they belong to me
but I am taking them nonetheless,
but when I gather them up to go,
they crumble to dust and sand.

"Everything crumbles," I say.
"What am I doing wrong?"

A woman, a guide in that place, answers –
"Dust or the scent of oranges?
You wonder why it is dust and not oranges."

As I hear her, I know she is reciting,
but where have I heard the verse?
There is a fragrance, just now,
eluding me.

I can almost scent it, like the oils, bitter and sweet,
the peel leaves on skin when you turn it back,
tiny droplets hanging suspended
in the air.

SHIVAH

Mourning, they say.
Grief.

But this is not grief.
This is the place between the worlds,
neither with the living nor the dead.

Life suspends all time
and the universe turns
on a tiny axis
of loss.

I'm fine, I tell my friends,
and it's true.
I'm only not entirely

Here.

Don't Breathe the Breath
of a Dead Man

Last night
I dreamed my daddy was alive.
We were on the phone,
and he was complaining about the air
in his hospital room —
too warm, perhaps, or too cold.

The air conditioning men were there,
but it still wasn't right.
There was some kind of opening in the ceiling or
walls, letting air and light in,
or out.

A crack like an orchid, cathedral ceiling,
hint of unfolding, of other...

I dreamed I was on the phone
and I was answering him,
talking to my daddy,
and Donna, my friend, looked at me
sharply.

Your father is dead, she said.
Why are you talking to him?

There was a man. Another man not my
daddy. In the way of dreams.
He was old. In fact, he was also dead.
A therapist, maybe.

I let him come close to me.
I don't know why, but I did.
I stood as he took me, working his way his hands
his mouth down my body, my left breast, my nipple
aroused.

I waited. I stood.
I only told myself,
it's okay, it's okay,
only don't let his breath touch you.
Don't breathe into yourself
the breath of the dead.

I woke, my head in pain.
A voice:
Find the girl
inside the room
inside the house
inside the walls.

BAD JEW

Don't want to go pray.
Don't want to beat my chest.
Don't want to hear that story again.
The Isaac one, when the angel
didn't make it in time,
and Isaac
died.

Stone for the blood,
stone heart. Never speak to God again.
Time to part.

Don't want to eat honey.
Don't want to dip bread.
Don't want to say hi to Daddy in his grave
before the opening
of the gates.

Only mercy. Only sin.
Only the way out and the way in.
Not for me.

Bad Jew.

DREAMS OF THE LAST FOUR DAYS

My father's body is on the ground.
Someone is pulling me away.
"But he's still warm," I say.

My mother's body is on the ground.
I get up in the middle of the night and
stumble across her in the hall.
We are lying across each other, tangled
and confused.
After a moment I realize she is warm,
only fallen.
Perhaps something is broken.
her leg is lying
at a funny angle.

I've been accepted into a university.
It's either Stanford or Rockefeller,
or some dreamish blend of both.
There is an auditorium, in New York,
where a Russian ballet troupe recently performed,
fittingly, someone shows me,
pointing out the Russian folk scene
painted on the velvet drop curtaining the stage.

All the other new students
are in the audience, celebrating with noisemakers,
masks, and cheers.
I realize how young they are,
how exuberant.

I wonder how it will be to be
an older student.

The sun is silent, I think at first, falsely.
I am seeking the solar wind.
It is a source, a tonic, or so I believe.
As I approach I realize how loud the sun is.
There is a roar beyond imagining,
the cacophony of the sun.

I wonder if I will be able
to withstand its song.

THE BASEMENT

There were stairs, down,
into the dark, and all its mysterious
machines.

My father in his element,
darkroom, model train,
sewing machine with its heavy,
wrought-iron pedal.

I learned to print, to make cording,
to wave at the small painted conductor
as the train went clicking down its track,
in circles on the table made of plywood
on two sawhorses.

He made furniture there, his mouth
full of tacks, and a hammer that was a magnet,
to pull them out, one by one.

Once, he told me, he'd swallowed one.
"What happened?" I asked,
but he shrugged it off.

He carried the sofas up the stairs
on his back, grinning as he sweated his way
up into the light.

THE TRUTH ABOUT SACRIFICE, OR, A POEM ABOUT INCARNATION
(9/25/01)

With what infinite tenderness
has the green leaf
been given its green?

And did the cries of feathered things,
the challenges, the mating call,
the territorial indignant shout
evolve so human ears and mind
could learn to sing?

How like the stones
is my blood: mineral, essential.

How precious is the rain.
But does it wash my tears,
or simply fall, unknowing?

Human, I, I know it.
I know the green, the song, the rain.

This is my life, here,
in all this beauty. A wind,
a breeze of air and night,
kisses me.

Who is the giver, and who the gift?

I will weep to leave this place.
Though they send me into light,

still I will turn,
and weep
for the joy it was
to have skin,
to be able
to tremble,

for the way my heart could feel,
even when it broke,

and for the way
every breath
was prayer.

Everything (12/6/01)

everything unravels

hearth, warren, babel,
pyre

the accidents of placement

the ones who slept late or
lingered
over coffee

the man who wrote an email to his wife.

his coworker left him there,
thinking him dazed but he
wouldn't come with her

he made it out but she still thinks
what if

and the city sleeps, dreaming
of ash
and vapors
and bones

and wakes to the words
"everything is okay;
we're strong, we're strong."

MEMORY ON THE ANNIVERSARY OF 9/11

It's not the headlines one remembers,
nor the worn images that bludgeoned us,
numb, shocked, grieving

edge of panic

It's the memory of the memory
of smoke

There is a curl that rides an ocean breeze
up the Hudson to where,
in my imagination,
I stand remotely on the shore — in my hand
a white flower

Meanwhile,
in the not-so-haiku world,
I wait for that day to come and go;
tune out the shrill politics of suffering and fear.
Behind me, a weight of thunder
presses my neck.
A whisper of a whisper
closes my throat:

"This is life."

RAISED A WARRIOR

What does the warrior raze
when rage departs, and war is ended,
and the tyranny of farmers
lays its bane?

The garlands turn to refuse soon enough.
Returning soldiers meet a wary gaze.
The killer is not welcomed at the hearth
and all his sacrificed innocence
is curtly mourned and then disdained

Then comes wisdom, washed in blood.
Then his feral dignity is turned,
his offering repealed,
and dark design must find release:
Beware the warrior with no home,
no comfort for his flayed and wounded heart.
No plowshares for his sword he'll beat,
nor, tasting now the rite of power
rough within him, will he
cherish peace.

PIECES

I don't know why it was
that particular image that got me.

We sat, social workers and psychs,
eating the same bad chicken cordon bleu
night after night in the medical school cafeteria
adjacent to the coroner's building.

The firemen mostly laughed, and told
stories, and complained about the food
(which had been donated by a local businessman),
occasionally going quiet, especially on the days
when they found one of their own.

Everyone stops, they said. In the coroner's.
Everyone stops. They stand at attention.
The body of the fallen comrade is carried in.
Maybe it's not a body. Maybe it's a finger,
or a ring that was on that finger.
Maybe it's a joke they remember
that that person used to tell, badly,
over beer.

The firemen and the cops,
the parole officers and prison guards,
the chaplains and the D-MORT team,
people flown in from all over the country
in 3-weeknon-stop stints.

Once, a well-meaning psych said solemnly
to the assembled diners at one table how moved

she was by the courage of the brave.
What incredible spirit it must take
to be willing to sacrifice health and possibly life
to rescue another.

"Fires are fun," the fireman said, his face reddening.
"I like what I do," he explained. It's not courage.

One day I asked a man I'd been talking with,
"Does this help any? Having us here like this?"
He thought about it and said,
"I can say the things I don't want to take home.
I can say them to you, and not my wife."

He told me quietly about what they'd found that day.
An intestine. Just that, all that was left
of a woman or a man.

The vulnerability of it shocked me,
as well it should.

I took it home, away from this man's family.
I can claim this one part — I kept this one harm
from those he loved.

I rocked all night on the couch,
cradling to myself
the delicacy and pain
of human incarnation.

DEATH

Maybe it's the way
a short poem
can be just as poignant and beautiful
as a long one.

You see the span
of the life
of someone you love
and it always feels too short.

But do you hold
a single flower
in less regard
than the garden it came from?

I am trying to unwind
this knot of pain.
I am trying to breathe
the beauty of this flower, this life,
whether it is "yesterday" or
"tomorrow" or "now."

It's still too short. I'm
not appeased.
Even so, life calls.

COLLAPSE/TODAY'S GRIEF

I keep thinking of hits,
of taking a hit:
first fear, then elation,
then the sucker-punch
of loss,
falling farther
than the seam they've dug,
and more black.
And the electric mad
possession, feelings
like a god within,
dangerous and cold.

I worry
for their electrolytes,
and for the ones who fainted,
and the ones whose trust
was skewered on a word.

There will be
some mad revenge:
like Oedipus
with spikes for eyes
or a fever spiked
with grief

THANATOPSIS

1.

Sooner or later, Vesuvius blows,
and we are left, seared with shock.
Either because we never thought
the ash would find us
in the middle of our pretty rooms
with painted walls,
with only enough time,
maybe, to reach and hold
one other person as we each
go down,

Or because we were the ones who got away,
an accidental sailing trip
or long before,
because that old mountain
never felt quite right, anyway,
and we left home, with arguments and pain,
and now are looking,
from very far away and through
grief thicker than the lingering smoke
at all we left behind.

2.

Sooner or later, Vesuvius blows
and you watch the shadow of its smoke
on a television screen,
while coffee percolates

and the bath water runs
and you only have time for a bite of toast
and it's time to go about your day.

At night, you send money on a website.
A few of your favorite artists sing songs that
wrench your heart (the miking, on the other hand,
isn't up to par, leaving you mildly disconcerted
in your charity and shame).

Disconcerted. Ha ha.

3.

Sooner or later, Vesuvius blows.
Poison dust falls out of the mail. Something
unwinds inside the tiniest part
of who you are. A virus, a sentience, a gene.

Sooner or later, your heart stops beating.
And all the rhythm of the world is lost.
And the music never was.

When I lost my heart
I thought
I would never walk again
into the world.

Pain sears us but it's never enough.
There is only so much we can learn, to prepare,

like holding your breath under water for as long
as you can. A child's trick; a child's hope,
to see what it's like. To survive the moment
of annihilation.

Sometimes I want to die, if only
to resolve this ambivalence, not knowing,
and feeling things both ways –
with faith, and with despair.

I say these words, knowing
they'll trigger some alarm.
But it is only the voices speaking.
Meanwhile,
the child descends once more
with reckless hope
and flagrant abandon.

The pool is all embrace.
This is life, the watcher says.
The child exhales and counts the bubbles
as they rise.

BEAUTIFUL PLANET

The plane flew lower
than I'm used to.
Recognizably down the Hudson,
the pilot pointing out
the World Trade Center site,
on the left side.

Brooklyn lay like a map of, well,
Brooklyn, Far Rockaway its farthest shore,
until the ocean billowed below us,
so close we could see the ruffling of the waves.

I must have dozed, because I don't remember
what was next.
But a while later, I looked again.

We were riding down the Chesapeake.
Inlets and marshes and streams winding like
dragons twisting and undulating to the sea.

Beautiful planet, I thought, and the light
was gentle and warm.

Near Newport News,
we passed the Ghost Shipyard,
Rusted toys lined neatly in the bay.
So warships rest, as do we all,
in time.

3

The Funky
Backdraft

~ *The first letter is silent.*

ALEPH BET

the first letter
is silent

There Is a Stopping Place

Sometimes, there is a massive place,
a stop,
so thick with waiting
that I don't even know
where, or who, or what
I am, or if

God is listening,
but only God as even
angels flare into this
fire, this mindless blinding
fire that has
no rhythm, no next

Of course from that place
no words scrape from mouth to air
This is
annotation not
annunciation

THE TORAH, OR, EPISTEMOLOGY

I am the silver hand
moving across the text.
There are no vowels.
To read this text,
you have to know what it says.

Ikebana

Beauty of the second flower
mars perfection of the whole, but
in itself, a universe of bloom

If I could pluck from time
the sundered flower...

But everything
is lost to the
Arrangement.

∿ *for Barb*

Barb's Book

It's so real her friend tells a story
in his own, published novel,
of her manuscript receiving
the highest advance ever granted
to a genre author.

A fortune teller, in Salem, no less,
witchily warns against men.
This is not taken
as literal.

8 months at the editor's desk,
and she dreams, not that it's sold,
but that it sold years ago, and is in
its seventh printing.

In the sequel, the characters
strain and struggle and dream.
They, too, intuit an end
in which happiness
is a thing long known,
and never squandered.

WRITER

Sometimes, the protocol trips her up.
Words misfile, or strangle, or change places
in a mischievous dance
between inspiration and execution.

The customs of this place are strange, milady, yes.
But she manages. She's well-seasoned, after all,
in these negotiations.
She gets through school, and boys, and
assignments abroad, adventures dark and bright
and the return back to familiar ground to find
true love with her glory hallelujah!
her beautiful girl.

She lives here. She really does.
Works and rents and cares for things.
And cats. And friends who love her,
whom she loves.

And all the while, the unstoppable calling,
not exactly siren but not exactly not,
like a symphony that drowns
or a solitary chime:
the revolutions and devices
of the worlds inside.

∾ *For Barb*

DOING IT

It certainly isn't choice.
It's not as if one day you wake up
and decide and then research the skills
and practice some
and go to a school, and then,
off you go,
and you're a writer.

You don't learn this,
though there are many things to learn,
along the way, to do it well.

You don't turn it off and on, either.
Vacation isn't when you don't do it.
Showers, neither, nor walking in the park
with nothing to write on, and no one in range
to tell your words to.

(The rocks listen quietly, but then,
what do rocks know of plot and dream?)

In some ways it's like a drug.
Especially the bad part, when you need it,
and your stomach itches, from the inside,
and your head is about to blow.

And then you sit, or pace, or however it goes.
You open the door in your mind,
or wherever it lives, for you,
and you say,

"Come."

∿ for Barb, Ruth, Janis, and Rhi

Violation

Some poems are almost
too intimate to read.
They curl inside you like the smoky
tongue of sex,
like something steaming up your leg
or dripping down.

They tease you like a finger,
horrifying, rude,
a stab that touches where you're starved.

Your fingers burn. The letters sting.
You feel the hollow
where your heart should be.
Or feel it full.

Like waking in another's dream,
only it's their body, and their grief,
and it leaves you stunned,
and it leaves you,
all alone.

Because it's done, suddenly.
And there's nothing more.
And you're supposed to just go on.

Only you don't.
Because you're gasping, or too tense.
Too recognized, too real.
Just one more breath, until release,
and the air is not enough,

and the silence drowns,
so hard to take, just out of reach,
trembling on the verge
of understanding and pain.

AND THAT'S HOW

Overheard on a New Jersey Transit bus:
"The girlfriends, they come
with their short skirts,
so their old man
can come in the front door.

"The guards know what's happenin'.
They look the other way.

"'Johnson!' they say,
'what you doing over there?'
They keep the other guys away
from the guys with girlfriends.

"She sits on his lap,
and he takes out his pipe,
hard and shiny as arithmetic.
And she's there,
taking it right up the front.

"And that's how prison babies are born."

The Funky Backdraft

This is not the well-tempered
poem.

This is not the gasping surrender,
the bliss of fixed design,
the happy meal prize
of revelation.

This is the funky backdraft,
the ungraceful grace.
This is the way
you're banging a stranger,
and the stranger is you.

The moment (or day, or life)
before it snaps into sense,
and you're just wandering around,
tangling with oblivion,
snapping at bugs, singing snatches of tunes
you can't sustain because you can't get it right
and you can't let it go.

Like a dream you know will change everything,
if only you remembered.

And there's a hunger gnawing inside
but nothing in the refrigerator is right,
and there, my friends, there in that feeling,
right there, in the worst of all of that,
that's where your poem lives,
that's where your dreaming lives.

In all the raw, in all the wrong.
Just hanging over the edge of something
that's just about to trip into the most
amazing light.
Just one thing left for you to do,
after the deep breath, and the whining
and the prayer, and the collapse to hopeless faith
that you'll never write again, never do anything
of merit,
never amount to anything at all,
right there, from as far inside of all of that
as you can stand,
Have mercy.

Have mercy on yourself.
Have mercy on everything —
the garbage and the noise,
the tantrums and the faint surrender.

Have mercy.
It's the only way through.
No shortcuts, no reveal.
Nothing matters. Nothing comes to terms.
This is your truth.
You might as well
be kind.

How to Eat a Poem

1. CHOMP

2. Nibble delicately.

3. Lie flat on your back.
Your lover feeds you bits,
on your tongue.
Perhaps a blindfold is involved.

4. Blow torch.
Burn it up.
After, inhale the smoke.
Rub your finger down your scorched
skin.
It's not, strictly, eating,
but is another way to consume
the word.

5. Dive in.
drown in it.
Rather than letting it enter you,
be entirely surrounded, drenched,
immersed.
You will have to find your own way
out again.

6. Of course not all is tidbits and porn.
Sometimes a poem is a stick, that pokes you.
Sometimes it is a lofty dream, and you have no
place in it.

Sometimes
you must tear yourself away.
Sometimes
you must tear a new place out of the world and
make it yours.
Then again,
that's life,
and not a poem.

7. Suck it down.
Sometimes (isn't it?), it's delicious,
to be on your knees.

8. Be like a baby
and spit it up again.
Make your mother sing to you.
Make someone pat your back,
while you play with the taste
once again
on your tongue.

9. There's no accounting for taste.
Aroma guides you, but you never know.
Make sure you try the savory ones,
as well as the sweet.
Make sure you sample
all the flavors
of the words.

10. There is always the needle,

right into the vein.

11. Lock yourself in a room.
Carefully partake
of your secret stash.

12. Crash the party.
A waiter walks around
with plates of word soufflé
and poem on a stick.
All you have to do
is wait.

13. Binge. Eat ravenously, gluttonously.
Smear bits of it into your mouth. Chew
with your mouth full. Eat the small crumbs
that have fallen down
onto the floor.

Afterwards,
burp loudly and pat your stomach
in satisfaction.

14. Eat only appetizers,
like haiku, or Bantu combinations.

When someone offers you a sonnet,
decline politely and tell them you're on a diet.

4

Bezalel's Ring

~ *There's a ladybug on the ceiling.*

SPRING SNOW

snow on daffodils –
a long train ride as it falls:
his smile, sweet and sad.

SNAP

sun finally clears
winter's lingering finger:
earth and mind snap wide

∽ *for Ruth*

LADYBUG

There was a ladybug on my ceiling the other day.

A ladybug. 19 floors up.
I looked up, dumbfounded.

"Spring is here!" I said, cheerily, puzzling it out,
looking toward the window
I had opened the night before,
for the first time in many months.

Still, I stood, staring.
Will she be all right?

It was time to go to work.
When I got home, the ladybug was gone.
I hope she had a nice day,
playing in my apartment.

A week later,
I still look up, wistfully,
at the spot.

SPRING

Does She,
like one of us,
like one of the surrendering women,
whimper softly at the first release
of winter's shackling cold?

Does She hesitate
to unfurl her blooms?

Too long She slept in icy chains:
She's found her comfort there,
and must be coaxed.

Come, then,
let us greet Her sweetly:
We will sing Her
into light.

My Mother Had a Baby

Spring came, and with it,
the dreams:

The Lord and Lady dressed in red,
and She, pregnant.

A woman with five children,
and the baby cried,
until I turned her on her belly on my knee,
and soothed her with upward motions
along her spine, my hand stroking slowly,
right to left.

I looked down and saw my nipples
turned dark from their usual pink.
A tarot reading from a friend:
"A birth awaits."

Last night I dreamed
my mother had a baby,
a beautiful baby girl.
"My mother is seventy, you know,"
I told a friend. "Isn't it amazing?"

Speaking further, I said, "Of course,
when the time comes," (I hesitated to say,
"when my mother dies")
... "she will be my daughter.
I will raise her. She will be mine."

Waking, I realize,
my mother had a baby,
and that baby
is me.

AFTER THE WAR:
IN MY MOTHER'S GARDEN

She planted everything there,
after the war.
Mimosa and dogwood,
maple and oak.
From a deep hollow
she called it, she made it.
From her mind's bloody graves
she wove a scent of roses.

A barefoot child
by the wild mulberry,
stained fingers, the fruit
nearly black.
The birds eat their fill
and pass it through,
almost unchanged.

Honeysuckle clings
to the side of the house,
and roses climb the rest,
tight-fisted fuchsia, languorous white,
generous pastels.
She gently strokes
the velvet and the thorn
like the face of a child.

Tending her garden,
refusing to prune,
planting violets from cuttings,
pussywillow from a stick.

We put everything in the ground
and some of it grows.
Seeds from apples and pears,
seeds from watermelon.

Not even a bee-sting
will make me wear shoes.

In the winter,
an albino blackbird
visits our garden
and eats the seeds
we have put in the snow.

THERE ARE PLACES

There are places that are home.
A sugar maple in the front yard,
its arms around me.
I watch the baseball games
across the street.
Nobody knows where I am.

The mountain at the music camp.
I step out alone from the practice rooms,
and listen to a higher singing
of the wind. It fills me with its lyric
for a long, long time.

Storms, over and over, on a trip to Santa Fe.
My mother is celebrating her 75th year.
The mountains are clashing with the clouds.
I feel alive.

In my bed, a lover's hand,
anchoring me to ground.
I'm sinking, so deep. The further in I go
the more it seems there is a welcome to my soul
in heat, in touch.
I tumble back, further, to a backyard,
blanket, earth, me, and sun, the sound
of a freight train in the distance,
calm and familiar.

Soon, my best friend
will come around
and ask me if I want to play.
The bikes are leaning against the wall.
There are bees in the roses, in the trees.
Later, I will lean out the window
in the upper story, breathing
the distant river air,
brushing honeysuckle pollen
from my thumb.

IMPATIENS

Driving in Jersey with Louisa
up to see the horses and from the car I say,
"Pretty flowers," and she says,
"Impatiens".

"What do you get
when you don't water the hydrangea?"
I retort.
"Dehydrangia."

We giggle and groan. She tells me
About Arabians, and a kind of very large horse
with a very broad back.

"No," she says, when I point again.
"Those aren't the same."

"They are," I insist. "Or at least,
impatiens-like flowers."

We howl and repeat the story to each other
for many years.
Over her broken shoulder as it mends,
and the horse that is slowly, carefully,
learning dressage, a penitent near-stallion
who fretted in the long months
in which she stayed away.

She loves him even when his recalcitrance
costs her so.

Sometimes it's the near-misses
that derange and arrange our lives.
Sometimes we tumble down,
broken, furious, scared of forgetting
why we're here,
scared of losing that ability to laugh,
as we fall.

He scents the apples in the pail.
She shows me how to hold my hand, flat,
like a plate. His breath is sweet,
his lips delicate and soft.

"Good boy," she says, and makes me touch
his velvet nose.

~ *for Louisa*

Poem on a Dream of Bees

Honey and sting its gifts.
Without it, fruition fails.

As for the buzzing,
I am both awakened
and disturbed.

I lie very still,
waiting for the fear
to pass.

Mama, the Vermillion Cliffs

Mama lays down on her back and lazily
grins up at the blue, blue sky,
old friend and lover.

Her wrinkly tits hang out of
her raggedy torn blouse

and she grins some more.
She doesn't mind the pink
of a little sunburn.

THUNDER

Cozy in my bed
Thunder wakes me through the night –
Cradled in a storm

Next Time (Autumn Poem)

Next time,
we'll do this right on the earth,
leaves for a blanket, flaky and brown,
the warm finger of the sun, poking
through cool autumn air,
our bellies gritty with dirt,
mouths hungry for each other.

After,
I'll sink right down into the clay.
I probably won't come up
'till Spring.

WINTER MOON, CITY MOON

Moon hangs behind banked haze
like the chalk-smudged thumbprint
of a lazy god.

East River laps against cement banks,
as cold settles in.

In alleys of light that comprise city sky,
Solstice beckons.

Razzberry at the Unseen Moon

And though
the truly penitent
would neither offend
nor seek to lay blame,
I, shorn of both arrogance and
shame,
and winnowed to a
transparent lambency of
holy grief,
purified and true,
nonetheless thumb my nose,
betimes,
at the unseen moon.

WINK

Moon winks through striated clouds,
like Venetian blinds
stretched across her face.

BEZALEL'S RING*

The rhythms of the dark and light of the year
teach us to watch for things in cycles.
The year turns, the day lengthens once more,
and we are saved.
The dark, too, has its time –
a time of turning in, of things that birth
only out of sight, in velvet blackness,
in silent yearning.

The light, too, has its time again.
Breathe. You, too, have arrived here, now.
A time of want. A time to be released.
A time of breaking through
the lethargy of time, of stumbling song,
of tripping into and out of shadow.
Blinking stupidly, at the same old sun.

Hello, sun.

This, too, shall pass.

---

*The story goes that King Solomon asked his artisan, Bezalel, to
make a ring for him that would be something he could look at in
good times and bad, and it would be equally relevant. Bezalel
made a ring composed of an acronym of the Hebrew letters that
stand for the words: "this, too, shall pass."

5

Mercy

∾ *One day, it will be clear that the holy of holies is you.*

25

If God Was in the Camps

If God was in the camps,
if He wore a yellow star,
He wore the silver studs as well;
insignia of power.

If ravaged lands explode along
a road of pain and ruin
what hellish rage is fostered
for the thousandth generation?

God: everywhere, yes.
But scattered just as we are,
In bullet-wielding children
and silent twinkling star.

But where the heart of madness is
there rests in equal measure
a balm of grace and gratitude
in life and in its treasure.

To bear it all in witness
and stay simple though it breaks you,
and consonant with all of this
to still ask love to claim you,

is to love God into wholeness
from the ragged edge of pain,
and from unflinching vision dark
find innocence again.

As If

It was as if
it was a thing
that came to live with us

and none of us wanted
to give it a name
but we gave it many names.

The way a husband and wife
speak of each other, to their child,
not as, my husband, my wife, but
your father, your mother.

It was as if
it was everyone's child

and it tore into the unborn children
our bodies never bore,
and it woke the dead, the strange,
the uncle we were afraid of,
the crazy old woman
with bad teeth.

Screaming and incomplete,
it was not polite.
It respected
none of us,
though it forced a way
for us to respect each other
and ourselves.

But we feared it,
and it touched
our fear.

As if we held,
an ugly child
and found our arms
bloody and raw,

even as we nursed it,
achingly.
Even as we rocked it,
and lay awake, after,
panting,
straining to learn again
the sound we make,
when we bless each other
and ourselves.

It was as if we found
these things
in the mirror of each other's eyes
and in the belly pit of our grief,
over and over touching each other
in this darkness,
over and over reaching to find
a common breath.
Straining for that word that would bring
release.

It's time to heal.
The mirror is broken

and put away.
Let daylight come.
it was only a dream,
dark thing though it was,
real though it was: it ends.

The child wakes.
and we are rapt,
here, finally,
in our connection.
We find, startled,
it was our own breath
that screamed so loudly
in the night.
It was our own name
we refused to hear
and the same name
that was the sound, finally,
of blessing and release.

This is a good thing,
this passage. A bloodied thing,
but a good thing nonetheless.
This is a child
that had to be born.

Sing. Gently, but sing.

Nightmare thoughts linger.
They will,
even so.

"And You Shall Love"

Do you love yourself?

Yes, but,
do you love yourself?
Not like a poor relation,
with an effort to be kind.
Being good about it.

Do you love yourself like a crush?
The way you wrote his initials
in your notebook, over and over,
with an arrow, the pierced heart
of your enchantment?

Do you love yourself
like Rumi loved his God,
Stumbling and drunk
as if every hour
were midnight or dawn?

Do you love yourself
so hard it hurts,
so true the very thought of losing you
could make you weep?

Do you love yourself broken?
With scraggly hair and dirty nails,
hanging on, for dear life?

Do you love yourself as you rise up,
as you lie down, as you go about your way?

Would you die,
if you didn't have you?

Have you woken yet,
from that awful dream,
the recursive bargain of self-hate
you made to stay alive?
Is this the deal-breaker, yet?

The angel abides
until one day
your will abides no more:
From nowhere you can name
the unleashed heart of fire ascends
and you are joined:

As full of scars
as grace.

"Beloved."
A voice is heard.
The voice is yours.

(This time it is the angel's turn
to laugh; even God's hidden name
prances and smiles.)

THE TASK OF LOVE

The task of love is hard.
To love means to face the ways
the world is not complete.
To love is to enter, without reserve,
this incompleteness
and kiss the darkness there, and the wounds,
and the sharp, bristled planes that sting and burn.

I have not gone alone into this dark,
but it took me so long to find my way,
to remember why I came here.
To feel how completely You loved me,
to let me go, and stumble, and forget,
as I had to, and cry for You.

To love is to remember how much I miss
the presence and the light of You.
To know that nowhere in this darkness,
the darkness of my descent,
can I know You as I wish
("or the game," I almost hear you say,
"would be up.")

The task of love is hard
but the gift of love is a mounting storm,
a flood that overrides despair,
an unrelenting tide;
once admitted, it cannot be refused,
even as it drowns the lamenting spirit's cries.
Even as it overruns the weary mind.

Such confusion, as the thing around me,
the thing I thought I was, dissolves.
Such fragmentary grace, arising into Light,
as the order breaks apart,
and chaos dances with my dreams.

Into this Unknowing
I would gladly fall...

LEAVE NO TRACE

The hardest thing is to let yourself
be fully absorbed,
and know that you will never be lost.

Leave no trace.

This you were given:
to recognize grace. To know
world without end.

Why, then, does your belly rumble?
A coil of panic, a militant
chaos in your gut?

*Do not feed
the tiger*

Descend to the place
you fear to love.
The place that grabs and writhes,
the place with ugly faces and strange
desires. That burns you in an acid fire.

This is the test: to incarnate,
as it were, into your own
nightmare and beast,

with all the love at your disposal,
and all your eyes awake.

Dark cave though it is,
it is the only entry
to the place
beyond the flames.

TAROT

3 amber beads tied together
on a string.
He picks them up and
touches them lightly in turn.
A large white tom
lays curled on the bed,
his ears and nose pink and delicate.
I look out the window.
On the sill, obstructing
the view, are postcards, pottery,
a schedule from the ballet,
recipes from magazines.
I would like to escape
this room of dreams.
Standing here, arms folded.
I would like to see
beyond the window.
On the table, a pot of tea
is cooling,
a strong odor of mint.
The cat, suspicious, eyes
me from the bed
as I take my seat.
Across from me, the man
smiles, and begins to
shuffle the deck.

MAYA

One day you awaken and still feel
as if the dream is in you enough to make
the waking world a blur
but not enough to travel further
in its coign.

One day you wake up,
can't shake a dream,
and stumble your way
through the daylight hours.

One day you wake,
can't shake (a dream).
You stumble —
(what was it?)

One day you wake,
so.

At night, no respite comes.
The dream is lost,
though a persistent finger
trails down your neck,
tickles at your spine
at the most inopportune
moments.

Falling, down, almost got it,
snorting, gone. Cough of frustration,
of almost (riding it over the edge),
of no.

Roll over, then, resign
to the unclarity of thought, of progress
through this so called reality,
this so called veil.

Outside the window,
life's atwitter.
The cat howls and the birds scramble,
loudly, in the bush.

SCARS

I hate my scars,
but they don't hate me.
I bitterly desire
the old, smooth curve my belly had,
before.

Now, it's dimpled and disjoined,
bisected by a great, corrugated line
that tugs me when I reach too far,
like a leash you can't see. Not only
on the surface of the skin,
but deep inside.

Remember how I held you, it says.
Remember how I hold you still.
I am your tether, keeping you
on this side of the line.

Time enough, in eternity's realm
for the lightness and the Light you seek.
Be here, now, tethered to
bone, blood, and scars.

This is what it is
to live.

ONE DAY

One day, you'll wake
to a distant singing,
as far as memory,
as close as pain,
as intimate as skin,
when you lick the salt
to taste the sea you refused
to wash away.

One day, it will be clear
that the holy of holies is you.
That there is nothing
more mysterious
than being alive.

Some say, it's just a prelude.
The real song
comes after.

I say, the miracle is now.
As sweet as breathing.
Listen, now, how the heart twangs
to keep its beat.

Until then, courage.
You'll need it, here,
until you learn to dance.
Until you've heard the song,
and the music takes you.

Things will seem pretty drastic,
meanwhile.

God, So To Speak

What's it mean
to be a god?

Does it mean I get wings,
or can fly by the sheer power
of my desire?

Do I get a halo, or light beams
shooting out of my fingers
or arcing out of my eyes?

Maybe I get a holy cunt,
and men howl when they come,
inside me, their bodies all lit up
like a Christmas tree.

That's some kundalini, Bubba!

I think being a god
is like being anything.
You find some definitional certainty
in a name, and that's comforting.

I think my body is an extraordinary design.
You know, special, just like everybody else.
I think my tits are beautiful. And my belly,
round and scarred.

I think being a goddess, which is to say a god
in woman form, is kind of cool, but after all
just another way to say that I'm alive.

Life: crazy, beautiful, aggravating — isn't it?
I'm so very, very grateful when the words come.
I know too well the not knowing, the not
very fun not knowing, not being able to name,
stuck in a bland ache of sameness,
of really nothing terribly wrong and yet,
that vague suspicion and desire, but it
all feels like whining and still wondering,
(not knowing) when the hell is my life really going
to begin.

I sit in my wee, sorry, lazybones way,
trying to "hold" the ennui and rage.
Some days I just grit my teeth
and the deepest breath I can manage is a snort,
just panting through the motions.
Goddess, god, demons and rogues — or just a
rhythm of snark?

So grateful, you see, for the days the words come.
Then, oh yeah, it's like finding the divine
right inside my little brain. And God said.
And there was.
And it was...

Very, very good.

And so it is. So it is,
when I remember. When all the stars line up
and my hormones cooperate
and it just goes ... *zing*.

(My heart reaches out to touch
the fool I am —
Love, the truest god I know,
laughs)

KOL HA'NESHAMA

∾ after David Whyte

I don't know what faith is,
but I know that the sun kisses my skin
and breath relaxes into "yes."

I don't know if tomorrow
the sun will rise (though it's generally
part of my plans.)
I don't know, really, if I'll live to tell the tale.
That's why, so often,
whispering is appropriate.

Prayer is a letter,
now more than ever, year after year,
intimate and abstract at the same time.
God is still the destination
without a zip code.
Maybe karma is another way of saying,
"return to sender" or "file not found."

Maybe the letter is always written
to ourselves, and we need the drama
of sending it away on a journey for a while.
(We sit, waiting for post-cards of affirmation,
view spectacular, natives charming,
heaven all the rage, wish you were here.)

The world opens,
moment by moment,
to sun, to light, to rain,
and then to dark.

One blink, and everything changes.
Meanwhile, in my mind,
I'm remembering sunlight,
hoping for it, for the coming day.
In my body, my breath carries on,
sometimes with this song of awakening and desire,
and sometimes, simply, faithfully,
without any attention paid to it at all.

I'm chagrined, realizing this,
knowing I'm certain to forget again.
Glad for whatever it is within me
that never does.

"all that has breath..."
(praises God)
which also translates to "everything alive."

A SECRET NAME FOR HOME

It happens so infrequently
and is incomplete, always incomplete.
Like the tension on the steering wheel,
wanting to look beyond the road's edge
at the beautiful water.
needing to keep my eyes
on the road.

A longing, a glimpse, at the waves.
The fillip of a dolphin's tale, arrowing away
from an oncoming cloud.
My head, aching from the coming rain
And the light, deep grey upon the waters,
which are going from translucence
to dusk.

A breath. Deliberate release of the grip
in my hands. The rock, on my left.
How close the tsunami will be, when it comes,
when it washes away this road I am traveling on,
this precious moment burned forever
in my memory,
of a place I can almost feel myself
at home in.

HOME

It took a long time.
It's almost hard to remember, now,
what it felt like, before things changed,
before I felt my body
as home.

Pain separated me, then,
from my sadness.
Sharp, distracting, clever.
A child in a dress-up gown
with a glittery wand,
and the sharp heel
of seduction and scorn.

Pain beckoned and I arrived,
tamed, at her feet,
shivering and lame.
It was transport. It was worship,
even as I mourned.

This body. This body. This love,
for the world. For me. For sharp light
on dew, on grass, ecstatic and cold.

"I want another body," I said,
moaning into the light. "I want to be free."

But I missed, later,
the lyricism of suffering.
I became
an ordinary girl.

It took a long time.
But I finally settled in.
The breath no longer stopping
at the tense barrier of my diaphragm.
My vision no longer locked
on a close horizon.

My body, warm, and slow,
and even with its scars and wounds,
complete.
Ready to receive,
ready to be received
into the world.

~ *for Selene*

MIDDLE AGE

You begin it, by knowing you'll die.
Not only do you know, but it's not so terrible.
In fact there is that first, faint hint
of a secret desire to be done,
finally, with loss.

Don't get me wrong. Acceptance
is hard won, after struggle and pain.
You might be one of those
who spends a panicked surge of seed,
of love, of hope,
as if attractiveness ends, here,
and must go out
in flames.

Eventually, though,
all that settles.
It really is easier, after all,
to look ahead with a steady eye.
No tomorrow is certain, therefore,
why not enjoy the day?

Slip curiously into night, as if to silk,
as if to play at a final surrender.
Pleasure mounts you like a dream;
so, like this, with practiced skill,
might you fall, with grace,
into the Light.

ACCIDENTAL MUSIC
(OF THE SPHERES)

It happens when I'm in the bath-tub,
my head back into the water.
Sound travels as if from another realm.

A secret silence, inside the sound,
which is a low vibration, and probably comes
from the rotating fan, sitting patiently
at the end of its extension cord,
in the hall.

To me, it's like the chanting of Tibetan monks,
the low, harmonic *om* of creation,
and a doorway inside me opens.

In New York, a high, wavering sound
falls like rain out of the air.
I'm stumped for quite a while, then one day
hear it for what it is: subway brakes,
piercing through the tunnels
as the train comes into the station..
The sound is harsh, but from a few blocks away,
abstracted across city streets,
it's angelic and sweet.

"Do you hear that?" I ask my friends.
They look at me, blankly.

There was also the year
it snowed in late spring,

and the only sound down Broadway
was the tinkling of chains on the wheels of buses.
That and the whoosh of cross-country skis.

If Heaven is a sound, then heaven is all around us.
I'll say it simply, yes, heaven is here.
I say it now, though not (too often) to my friends.
Inside the vibration of the simplest things.
Even the machines, even the paragons
of the artifice of man
can't help but participate. Everything is singing.
Everything is alive.

And it's private, or shy, or very calm.
You have to be willing
to put your head back, into the water.
You have to be willing to stop, suddenly,
in the midst of purchasing fruit,
in the midst of wondering
where you put your snow boots.

Hear the chanting, the sleigh bells, the choir.
The doorway opens, then, inside you.
And every accidental music
tunes you to its key.

THE 11ᵀᴴ SEPHIRA

I'd like to die at a
ripe old age.
Ripe like fruit, not fish.

I'd like to go like one of those
exploding hallucinogenic happy
flowers on Star Trek.
The one that makes Spock laugh.

I'd like to seed myself in the wind,
and everyone who saw me
would make a wish.

I'd like my last exhale
to be easy. To slide out of my throat.
To finally get it about *Tonglen*,
and letting go, and love.

I'd like to ride out
in a wave of bliss.
To be eager, like a bride.

I'd like to glimpse
The Sabbath Queen,
coming to meet me
at the margins of the field.

And all around
the singing of the trees,
angels descending
to a thousand invitations,
and the Soul, jumping out of its skin,
so to speak.

∽ *for Janis*

Every Culture Has Its Way

The motorcyclist has his wheels
The freedom of the road appeals

Monks will chant, and Christians pray.
The literati have their day
with turns of phrase
becoming paroxysms of faint praise

A punker loves the brilliant hue
of his inorganically crafted 'do

A Wiccan lays her circle clear
invoking forces far and near

Among the Jews I find my home
The Jewish mantra is the moan.

Spring Is Waiting for You

Spring is waiting for you,
bluebirds in the valley,
sun glancing off lingering snow,
beneath the ice, beneath the cold,
a quiet, potent, silvery triumph,
like a shout held in,
because the moment is too perfect
to disturb.

Spring is waiting for you,
mysterious and strange,
fulsome in the loam,
full of crawlies and wingies,
and fuzzies and whir,
slippy slidey pebbles floating
down the melting stream,
and little eggs popping open,
tadpoles and birdies,
tendrils of the shoots and seeds,
and there is disorder in the order,
and Goddess weeps crystal dew
for you to bathe your feet in.

Spring is waiting for you,
the way a lid lifts off the sky,
and it expands,
and a breeze floats in,
and you can breathe, in a different way,
because there is more space inside you,
space for Spring to unfold.

And it's in you and out and big and small,
pebble and sky and crawling things
and prayer and dancing and that shout,
finally, at the way it all dissolves, the way the light
dissolves the dust —
seed to seed, bone to bone, dust to dust —
waiting to set it all free

                  ∿ *for Ann*

ICE STORM

One year there was an ice storm,
and the dogwood, such a favorite in the spring,
was sheathed in ice.

Not knowing better, I counted it as wonder,
while adults worried and fussed
about broken branches.

The ice, I felt,
was blanket, not pain.
The tree was entirely sealed,
down to the smallest twig,
and was translucent in the light.

No worries, no worries.

This was winter,
before I knew
what winter was.

Yesterday,
I wrote a poem about spring
for a friend, dying in Ohio.
I put bluebirds in it, and skies she could
breathe in.

I let it go without much toil.
Spring comes quickly, sometimes,
if you know what I mean.

Last night, I remembered —

I have a body, and my body has desires.
I sat back, watching,
as toes spoke in wiggles,
as tides rose and ebbed inside me,
belly, throat, and eyes,
all speaking in their voices
of bubble and prickle and warm,
and I was breathing, breathing,
from the inside.
And I was lifted, slowly,
to a soft release.

I did not interfere.

For a time, the bluebirds sang,
and the sheathed tree glimmered
in the light.

Fragments of Mercy

There is no need, finally,
for the sacrificed heart.

I will be broken, soon,
and Something,
some thing of ash and wings and rain,
will rise.

Oh let me not wake
nor find my way
until the time is ripe
for being found:

For ecstasy,
forgiveness,
fire,
peace.

Mercy Crosses the Line

He begins as a Buddhist saint.
One day he travels, with a bunch of monks,
to China, where he begins to play with
girls' clothing.

His breasts still small, he poses,
one knee up, the other swinging.
Being a girl is nice, so one day

She has her hair done,
puts on a beautiful robe,
and is a Lady,
aristocratic, serene.

In her hands,
a willow branch, a flower, or a cup.
She stands on the head of a Dragon,
or sits a Lotus throne.

Sometimes, she remembers
the monks, and the road she took to get here,
India to China,
Aveloketeshvara to Quan Yin,
male to female,
boddhisattva to Lady, to Goddess.
It's all in light, it's all in love.
So gentle, so gentle.
Compassion wears many faces,
she thinks to herself, and smiles.

Serenade

Sometimes you have to know
when to close your eyes.

The sweet fire burns
and the day draws to a close.

It will all be here another day,
with or without your watchful gaze.

Take comfort, you aren't needed here.
Which is not to say you have no place.

You'll ponder this all night, I know.
Better still, rest, and dream.

The candle's burning,
and only your breath
is as flickering, or as warm.

Dvorah Simon was born in Delaware to
Hungarian Jewish parents. She was
introduced to poetry by way of Milne and
Christopher Robin; "The King's
Breakfast" was a particular favorite,
especially as acted out with her mother
and sister. She was also deeply moved by
the rhythms and imaginative power of
Hebrew liturgy, as well as the masterful
poetry of Rilke, Neruda, Rumi,
Ferlinghetti, and Oliver. When not
writing poetry or cavorting with friends,
Dvorah works as a clinical psychologist.
Dvorah teaches *Words Rise Up From Silence*,
a poetry-writing workshop focused on the
sensual qualities of words. She can be
contacted at dvorahpoetry@gmail.com.

OTHER BOOKS FROM
HANFORD MEAD PUBLISHERS, INC.

Through Thunder: An Epic Poem of Death and Rebirth by Tav Sparks In the midst of his stormy years and dark night of the soul, twenty years ago, Tav Sparks spontaneously wrote this 'epic' poem, *Through Thunder*. In phases the poem feels and sounds us through the archetypal "Hero's Journey" described by Joseph Campbell. It draws the perennial, turbulent, death-rebirth map of psychospiritual awakening, a process experienced by the mystics of all religions.

SoulCollage®: An Intuitive Collage Process for Individuals and Groups by Seena B. Frost. *Today's Librarian* called this book an "exciting, spiritual 'craft' book for making personalized Tarot-like cards." Unlike Tarot, Soulcollage® cards are personal, made with images people select intuitively from magazines and photos and together as a deck they create

a visual journal. Simple directions enable anyone to create a beautiful deck of cards that has deep personal meaning. SoulCollage is a satisfying artistic way to inner exporation, and to encourage identification and expression of inner feelings in educational, spiritual, or therapeutic group settings. It is fun, too. More than 200 examples of cards are included in the book. CDs by the author are available too.

SoulCollage® Card Pack - These 12 blank cards make it easy to begin creating one's own personal SoulCollage® deck. Made of quality matboard, these blank cards are professionally cut to the 5 x 8 inch size.

www.hanfordmead.com
www.soulcollage.com